the cocktail
hour

the
cocktail
hour

ben reed

photography by william lingwood

RYLAND
PETERS
& SMALL

LONDON NEW YORK

Senior Designer Susan Downing
Editor Miriam Hyslop
Production Tamsin Curwood
Art Director Gabriella Le Grazie
Publishing Director Alison Starling

Mixologist Ben Reed
Stylist Helen Trent

First published in the United States in 2002
by Ryland Peters & Small, Inc.
519 Broadway
5th Floor
New York NY 10012
www.rylandpeters.com

10 9 8 7 6 5 4 3 2 1

Library of Congress Cataloging-in-Publication Data

Reed, Ben.
    The cocktail hour / Ben Reed ; photography by William Lingwood.
        p. cm.
    Includes index.
    ISBN 1-84172-322-3
        1. Cocktails. I. Title.

TX951 .R355 2002
641.8'74--dc21   2002024850

contents

the cocktail hour

The origin of the cocktail is steeped in colorful myth. It has a number of explanations for its derivation. Among my favorites is the story of the publican who, during the American War of Independence, lost one of his finest fighting cockerels. He was inconsolable until the day an army lieutenant came riding into town with the bird. The publican immediately mixed up a special concoction (no doubt containing Kentucky whiskey) and served it to the soldier, toasting him with the phrase "to the cock's tail' (for returning the bird with all the feathers in its tail intact).

Although many of the cocktails we regard today as "classic" were invented before the 20th century, it was during the Roaring Twenties that cocktails came into their own. Immortalized on the silver screen, with dialogue laced with references to champagne cocktails and martinis, they became the drink of the chic and sophisticated. Ironically, it was prohibition and the abundance of bootleg or bathtub liquor that forced the alcohol-friendly masses to invent mixes, which first took the sting out of the illicit spirits and then confused the authorities raiding the speakeasies.

Today, the true classic is a drink of subtlety and depth of taste, where one ingredient perfectly complements another to create an elixir of no more than two alcoholic ingredients.

The methods of preparation are often hugely contentious—think martini with the ubiquitous "shaken" or "stirred" argument. Invariably, and this is the joy with timeless cocktails, when a cocktail can be made in a number of ways, a new title is often bestowed upon the drink and a new life given!

As cocktails evolve, we, as the drinks enthusiasts of the world, should always cherish the classic, because it gives us the foundation to both toast the past and mix for the future.

EQUIPMENT

The first thing any aspiring bartender should acquire is a **measure (jigger)**. Too many professional bartenders regard the jigger as a tool for the novice—their guesswork results in many delicate cocktails being ruined. The modern dual-measure jigger measures both 2 oz. and 1 oz. (a double and a single measure). The **shaker** is the second most important piece of equipment for a bartender. The **barspoon**, with its long spiraling handle, is useful for stirring drinks and for the gentle pouring required for layered drinks. The "wrong," flat end can

equipment
and
techniques

be used for muddling or crushing herbs, etc. A **muddler**, a wooden pestle for mixing or crushing sugar cubes, limes, and herbs, etc, and the **bartender's friend** for opening cans and removing corks and bottle caps, are also handy. A **mixing glass** with strainer is used for making drinks that are stirred, not shaken. Other useful but non-essential accessories include an **ice bucket, ice tongs**, and a **juice squeezer**.

GLASSES

The traditional **martini glass** is a very familiar icon, with its open face and slim stem. The **cocktail glass** is similar to the martini glass but with a slightly rounded bowl. The **rocks** or **old-fashioned glass** is a squat, straight-sided glass, which sits on a heavy base and feels comfortable in the hand. The **highball** and **collins** glasses come in various sizes, but they are all tall, slim glasses, designed to keep a long drink fresh and cold. The small, sturdy **shot glass** is designed with one purpose: getting the drink from one's glass into one's mouth with minimal fuss. The **champagne flute** is perfect for keeping the sparkle in your champagne cocktails. It should be elegant and long-stemmed, with a narrow rim to enhance the delicacy of the drink.

TECHNIQUES

There are six basic ways of creating a cocktail: **building, blending, shaking, stirring over ice, layering**, and **muddling.** Whichever method you are using, accurately measure the ingredients first to get that all-important balance of tastes right. If you would rather try guesswork, just see how much practice it takes to get the quantity right to fill the glass exactly—I still have problems in that department! The process of **building** a cocktail just requires adding the measured ingredients to the appropriate glass, with ice, and giving it a quick stir before serving. The **blending** method involves pouring all the ingredients into a blender, adding crushed ice, and flicking the switch. Using a **shaker** is the most enjoyable way to mix a cocktail, both for you and your guests. Add the ingredients to the shaker and fill it with ice. The shaking movement should be sharp and fairly assertive, but do remember to keep your hands on both parts of the shaker or at least a finger on the cap. Drinks containing egg white, cream, and juices should be shaken for slightly longer than the usual ten seconds. **Stirring** is the best method when you want to retain the clarity and strength of the spirits. Manhattans, for example, are always stirred. Use an ice-filled mixing glass and stir carefully to avoid chipping the ice and diluting the drink. Frost your serving glasses by leaving them in the freezer for an hour before use. **Layering** is the technique used for drinks such as the White Russian. With the flat end of a barspoon resting on the surface of the base spirit, pour each of the remaining spirits in turn down the handle of the spoon. This keeps the ingredients separate and allows them to be tasted one at a time. The **muddling** technique involves using the flat end of a barspoon or a muddler to mix or crush ingredients and allow the flavors to be released gently.

Pink Gin is a thoroughly British cocktail that deserves a premium gin. Although it originated as a medicinal potion in the British Navy, Pink Gin became one of the most stylish drinks in 1940s' London.

pink
gin

2 oz. gin
a dash of Angostura bitters

Rinse a frosted sherry or martini glass with Angostura bitters, add chilled gin, and serve.

GIN

classic
dry
martini

2 oz. gin
a dash of dry vermouth
green olive

Using a mixing glass, chill
the gin and vermouth over
ice, and pour into a frosted
martini glass. Garnish with
a green olive.

The **Classic Dry Martini** has long been considered the ultimate in sophistication and elegance. Its roots date back as far as the 1840s, where it is believed to have been served at a bar in Martinez, California. The **FDR** (named after President Roosevelt) and the **Smoky Martini** are popular variations on the stylish classic.

fdr
martini

ALSO KNOWN AS THE DIRTY MARTINI
2 oz. gin
a dash of dry vermouth
½ oz. olive brine
green olive

Add the gin, a dash of dry vermouth, and the olive brine to a shaker filled with cracked ice. Shake sharply and strain into a frosted martini glass. Garnish with an olive. Made to Mr. Roosevelt's specifications!

smoky
martini

2 oz. gin
a dash of dry vermouth
a dash of whiskey

This is a variation on the FDR Martini, with the whiskey substituting for the olive brine, but the method is identical.

silver
bronx

2 oz. gin
a dash of dry vermouth
a dash of sweet vermouth
2 oz. fresh orange juice
1 egg white

Shake all the ingredients
vigorously over ice and strain
into a chilled cocktail glass.

golden
bronx

The method is the same as
above, but substitute an egg yolk
for the egg white.

The **Bronx** dates back to the
days of Prohibition, when gang
bosses reigned and booze played
an important part in the economy
of the underworld. Different areas
of New York became known
for the special cocktails they
offered, such as this speciality
of the Bronx. Like the Manhattan,
it has three variations: the dry, the
sweet, and the perfect. The **Silver**
and **Golden Bronx** are variations
on the perfect, with the addition
of egg white or egg yolk.

gin gimlet

2 oz. gin
1 oz. lime cordial

Pour the gin and cordial into a shaker filled with ice. Shake very sharply and pour through a strainer into a frosted martini glass.

Made popular during in the 1930s, the **Gin Gimlet** should be shaken vigorously to make sure the cocktail is chilled to perfection, then strained carefully before serving to catch any chips of ice. The **Journalist**, another classic gin cocktail, is a good pre-dinner drink to order at a bar. If you are making a Journalist at home, watch the measurements carefully; it's a drink that needs to be very finely balanced.

the
journalist

1 oz. gin

a dash of sweet vermouth

a dash of dry vermouth

2 dashes of fresh lemon juice

2 dashes of triple sec

2 dashes of Angostura bitters

Shake all the ingredients over ice
and strain into a frosted martini glass.

Two offshoots of the original Gin Fizz, (a classic that some would say should remain untouched), these cocktails have now become classics in their own right. The substitution of champagne for the club soda in the **Royal Gin Fizz** helps to make it special and lends it a little extra fizz (surely no harm there!). The addition of the rose flower water in the **New Orleans** or **Ramos Fizz** accentuates the juniper flavor in the gin, and the dash of cream gives this very light drink a little more body.

royal gin fizz

2 oz. gin
1 oz. fresh lemon juice
1 barspoon white sugar
  (or 1 oz. sugar syrup)
champagne
1 egg white

Put the egg white, gin, lemon juice, and sugar into a shaker filled with ice and shake vigorously. Strain into a collins glass filled with ice. Top with champagne.

new orleans fizz

ALSO KNOWN AS THE RAMOS FIZZ

2 oz. gin
1 oz. fresh lemon juice
1 barspoon white sugar
  (or 1 oz. sugar syrup)
1 oz. rose flower water
  (or orange flower water)
1 oz. light cream
a dash of egg white
club soda

Add all the ingredients, except the soda water, to a shaker filled with ice. Shake vigorously and strain into a highball glass over ice. Gently add the club soda, stirring with a barspoon while doing so.

VODKA

The **Black** and **White Russians** are classics that have been on the scene since the Cold War era. They make stylish after-dinner cocktails with their sweet coffee flavor, which is sharpened up by the vodka. The White Russian, with its addition of the cream float, is even more appropriate as a nightcap.

black russian

2 oz. vodka
1 oz. Kahlúa coffee liqueur
stemmed cherry

Shake the vodka and Kahlúa together over ice and strain into a rocks glass filled with ice. Garnish with a stemmed cherry.

white
russian

For a White Russian, layer 1 oz. light cream
into the glass of a Black Russian over the back
of a barspoon. Garnish with a stemmed cherry.

silver
streak

1 oz. chilled vodka
1 oz. kümmel

Pour a generous single measure
of chilled vodka into a rocks glass
filled with ice. Add a similar amount
of kümmel, stir gently, and serve.

A classic in its own right, the first **Vodkatini** dates back to the 1950s. As with the Classic Dry Martini, there are four important things to consider when it comes to making it: the quantity of vermouth, to shake or stir, straight up or on the rocks, and finally, an olive or a twist. The **Silver Streak** features the liqueur kümmel and has a distinctive, aniseedlike taste that comes from the caraway seeds used in its production.

vodkatini

2 oz. vodka
a dash of dry vermouth
pitted olive or lemon zest

Fill a mixing glass with ice and stir with a barspoon until the glass is chilled. Tip the water out and top with ice. Add a dash of dry vermouth and continue stirring. Strain the liquid away and top with ice. Add a large measure of vodka and stir in a continuous circular motion until the vodka is thoroughly chilled (taking care not to chip the ice and dilute the vodka). Strain into a frosted martini glass and garnish with either a pitted olive or a twist of lemon zest.

2 oz. vodka
1 oz. Galliano
fresh orange juice
orange slice

Pour a large measure of vodka
into a highball glass filled with
ice. Fill the glass almost to the
top with orange juice and pour
in a float of Galliano. Garnish
with an orange slice, and serve
with a swizzle stick and straw.

harvey
wallbanger

The story goes that Harvey, a California surfer who had performed particularly badly in an important contest, visited his local bar to drown his sorrows. He ordered his usual screwdriver— only to decide that it wasn't strong enough for what he had in mind. Scanning the bar for something to boost his drink, his eyes fell on the distinctively shaped Galliano bottle, a shot of which was then added to his drink as a float. Needless to say, his resultant state after a few of these was so rocky that, as he searched for the door on the way out, he bounced off a couple of walls before spilling out onto the street. Harvey Wallbanger, they called him.

moscow
mule

2 oz. vodka
1 lime
ginger beer

Pour a large measure of vodka
into a highball filled with ice.
Cut the lime into quarters,
squeeze, and drop into the glass.
Top with ginger beer and stir with
a barspoon. Serve with a straw.

The creation of the **Moscow Mule** celebrates the godsend
that is ginger beer. It lends the Mule its legendary kick and an
easy spiciness. The **Bloody Mary** has been a renowned hang-
over cure or pick-me-up for years. Curing hangovers can be
painless, and should be enjoyable, too. They are an aspect of
bartending that cannot be ignored—and, in a truly biblical
way, what the bartender giveth, so shall he take away.

bloody
mary

2 oz. vodka
8 oz. tomato juice
2 grinds of black pepper
2 dashes of Worcestershire sauce
2 dashes of Tabasco sauce
2 dashes of fresh lemon juice
1 barspoon horseradish sauce
1 celery stick

Shake all the ingredients over ice and strain
into a highball glass filled with ice. Garnish
with a celery stick. (These measurements
depend on personal tastes for spices.)

WHISKEY

The naming of Manhattan Island has an anecdotal history that links it with the cocktail. "Manhachtanienck," which roughly translates as "the island where we became intoxicated," so named in the early 17th century by Lenape Indians after drinking a dark spirit.

2 oz. rye
1 oz. dry vermouth
a dash of Angostura bitters
lemon zest

dry manhattan

For each of the variations, add the ingredients to a mixing glass filled with ice (make sure all ingredients are very cold) and stir the mixture until chilled. Strain into a frosted martini glass, add the garnish, and serve.

perfect
manhattan

2 oz. rye
½ oz. sweet vermouth
½ oz. dry vermouth
a dash of Angostura bitters
maraschino cherry

sweet
manhattan

2 oz. rye
1 oz. sweet vermouth
a dash of orange bitters
orange zest

old fashioned

2 oz. bourbon
1 white sugar cube
2 dashes of orange bitters
orange zest

Place the sugar cube soaked with orange bitters into a rocks glass, muddle the mixture with a barspoon, and add a dash of bourbon and a couple of ice cubes. Keep adding ice and bourbon and keep muddling until the full 2 oz. has been added to the glass (making sure the sugar has dissolved.) Rim the glass with a strip of orange and drop it into the glass.

The **Old Fashioned,** the **Mint Julep,** and the **Rusty Nail** have one thing in common—they are all timeless whiskey cocktails that never fail to delight. As those among us who are already connoisseurs of the water of life will tell you, each cocktail should be serenaded with a few gentle words of seduction, sipped, and finally, savored.

mint julep

2 oz. bourbon
2 sugar cubes
5 sprigs of mint

Crush the mint and sugar cubes in the bottom of a collins glass. Fill the glass with crushed ice and add the bourbon. Stir the mixture vigorously with a barspoon and serve.

rusty nail

1 oz. whiskey
1 oz. Drambuie
orange zest

Add both ingredients to a glass filled with ice and muddle with a barspoon. Garnish with a zest of orange.

boston
sour

2 oz. bourbon
1 oz. fresh lemon juice
2 barspoons sugar syrup
2 dashes of Angostura bitters
a dash of egg white
lemon slice and maraschino cherry

Add all the ingredients to a shaker filled
with ice and shake sharply. Strain the
contents into an old-fashioned glass
filled with ice; garnish with a lemon
slice and a maraschino cherry.

new orleans
sazerac

2 oz. bourbon
1 oz. Pernod
1 sugar cube
a dash of Angostura
  bitters

Rinse an old-
fashioned glass with
Pernod and discard
the Pernod. Put the
sugar in the glass,
saturate with
Angostura bitters,
then add ice cubes
and the bourbon
and serve.

Reputed to be the very first cocktail, the **Sazerac** has been around since the 1830s. To enjoy its flavors fully, drink it undiluted. The classic Sour is made with Scotch whiskey, but since I like my sours a little on the sweet side, I prefer the vanilla sweetness of this bourbon-based **Boston Sour**.

The **Hot Toddy**, with its warming blend of spices and sweet honey aroma, has long been the perfect comforter and will soothe any aches, snuffles, and alcohol withdrawal symptoms that your illness may have inflicted upon you. It's also a great life-saver for cold afternoons spent outside watching sports. Next time you have need to pack a thermos flask of coffee, think again—mix up a batch of Hot Toddies, and see how much more popular you are than the next spectator!

hot toddy

2 oz. whiskey

1 oz. fresh lemon juice

2 barspoons honey or sugar syrup

3 oz. hot water

1 cinnamon stick

5 whole cloves

2 lemon slices

Spear the cloves into the lemon slices and add them to a heatproof glass or a toddy glass along with the rest of the ingredients.

The **Mai Tai** was originally made in the 1940s by Victor Bergeron (Trader Vic) in California. With its complex mixture of flavors it has as many variations as it has garnishes. The one thing that most bartenders seem to agree on is that a thick, dark rum should be used, along with all the fruit-based ingredients that lend the classic its legendary fruitiness.

RUM, TEQUILA, & CACHAÇA

mai tai

1 oz. Demerara rum
1 oz. gold rum
1 oz. orange curaçao
½ oz. apricot brandy
½ oz. fresh lemon or lime juice
a dash of Angostura bitters
2 dashes of orgeat syrup
2 oz. fresh pineapple juice
a mint sprig

Add all the ingredients to
a cocktail shaker filled with
ice, shake and strain into
an ice-filled old-fashioned
glass. Garnish with a
pineapple slice and a mint
sprig. Serve with straws.

orange
daiquiri

2 oz. Creole Schrubb rum

1 oz. fresh lemon juice

2 barspoons sugar syrup

Measure all the ingredients and pour into an ice-filled shaker. Shake and strain into a frosted martini glass.

2 oz. golden rum

1 oz. fresh lime juice

3 barspoons sugar syrup

Measure all the ingredients and pour into an ice-filled shaker. Shake and strain into a frosted martini glass.

original
daiquiri

bacardi
cocktail

2 oz. Bacardi white rum
a dash of grenadine
juice of 1 small lime
1 barspoon of powdered sugar or
    a dash of sugar syrup

Shake all the ingredients sharply
over ice, then strain into a frosted
martini glass and serve.

The **Original Daiquiri** is a classic cocktail that was made famous in the El Floridita restaurant in Havana early in the 20th century. It has as many recipe variations as famous drinkers (Hemingway always ordered doubles at El Floridita), but once you have found the perfect balance, stick to those measurements exactly. The **Orange Daiquiri** and **Bacardi Cocktail** are two of the best-known variations.

A sweet, creamy drink that, for a time, epitomized the kind of cocktail disapproved of by "real" cocktail drinkers (compare a **Piña Colada** with a Classic Dry Martini!). However, since its creation in the 1970s, it has won widespread popularity, and now that we are in the new millennium, cocktails are for everyone, so there's no shame in ordering this modern-day classic at the bar.

piña colada

2 oz. golden rum
1 oz. coconut cream
½ oz. cream
½ oz. fresh pineapple juice
a slice of pineapple

Put all the ingredients into a blender, add a scoop of crushed ice, and blend. Pour into a sour or collins glass and garnish with a slice of pineapple.

rum runner

1 oz. white rum
1 oz. dark rum
juice of 1 lime
a dash of sugar syrup
6 oz. fresh pineapple juice

Shake all the ingredients sharply over ice in a shaker and strain into a highball glass filled with crushed ice.

The **Rum Runner** is a perfect example of rum's affinity with fresh juices.

Rum also has the ability to hold its own when combined with quite a selection

of other flavors. The **Planter's Punch** recipe can never be forgotten since

Myers has very kindly put the recipe on the back label of its rum bottle.

A great favorite for parties because it can be made in advance, Planter's Punch

can be prepared in an old oak barrel for authenticity, but a big bowl will do,

with slices of fruit, such as oranges, melons, apples, and pears, added.

The **T-Punch** is a refreshing drink, perfect for a hot summer day, and can be

made according to taste with more lime or more sugar for a quick variation.

planter's
punch

2 oz. Myers rum
juice of half a lemon
2 oz. fresh orange juice
a dash of sugar syrup
club soda
orange slice

Pour all the ingredients, except
the club soda, into a cocktail shaker
filled with ice, shake, and strain into
a ice-filled highball glass. Top up
with club soda and garnish with a
slice of orange.

t-punch

2 oz. white rum
1 lime
1 brown sugar cube
club soda

Place the sugar cube in the
bottom of an old-fashioned
glass. Cut the lime into
eighths, squeeze, and drop
into the glass. Crush gently
with a pestle to break up the
sugar. Add the rum and ice,
then top up with club soda.
Stir and serve.

The **Mojito**, with its alluring mix of mint and rum, invariably whisks its drinker away to warmer climes. Championed by Hemmingway in the 1940s and wildly popular in Miami for years, this Cuban concoction can now be found gracing the menus of discerning cocktail bars around the world.

mojito

2 oz. golden rum
5 sprigs of mint
2 dashes of sugar syrup
a dash of fresh lime juice
club soda

Put the mint into a highball glass, add the rum, lime juice, and sugar syrup, and crush with a barspoon until the aroma of the mint is released. Add the crushed ice and stir vigorously until the mixture and the mint are spread evenly. Top with club soda and stir again. Serve with straws.

cuba
libre

2 oz. white rum
1 lime
cola

Pour the rum into a highball
glass filled with ice; cut a
lime into eighths, squeeze,
and drop the wedges into
the glass. Top with cola and
serve with straws.

One of the most famous of all rum-based drinks, the **Cuba Libra** was reputed to have been invented by an army officer in Cuba shortly after Coca-Cola was first produced in the 1890s. Cachaça, a spirit indigenous to Brazil, is distilled directly from the juice of sugarcane, unlike white rum, which is usually distilled from molasses. The **Caipirinha** has made cachaça popular in many countries.

caipirinha

2 oz. cachaça
1 lime
2 brown sugar cubes

Cut the lime into eighths, squeeze, and place in an old-fashioned glass with the sugar cubes, then crush well with a pestle. Fill the glass with crushed ice and add the cachaça. Stir vigorously and serve with a straw.

2 oz. gold tequila
2 oz. champagne (chilled)

Pour both the tequila and the chilled champagne into a highball glass with a sturdy base. Hold a napkin over the glass (sealing the liquid inside), sharply slam the glass down on a stable surface, and drink in one go while it's fizzing.

tequila
slammer

margarita

2 oz. gold tequila
1 oz. triple sec (or Cointreau)
juice of half a lime

Shake all the ingredients
sharply with cracked ice.
Strain into a chilled cocktail
glass rimmed with salt.

The **Margarita** is the cocktail most closely associated with

tequila. This is the classic recipe, but when you are making

it at home there is no right or wrong way—just your way!

You can use Cointreau or triple sec, lime or lemon juice, or

even cordial, but never, ever use a readymade mix.

The **Tequila Slammer** is a drink that needs to be handled

with care. This one is more likely to be imbibed for the

sensation rather than the taste!

BRANDY, LIQUEURS, & APERITIFS

brandy
alexander

2 oz. brandy
½ oz. crème de cacao
  (dark and white)
½ oz. heavy cream
nutmeg

Shake all the ingredients over
ice and strain into a frosted
martini glass. Garnish with
a sprinkle of nutmeg.

The **Brandy Alexander** is the perfect after-dinner cocktail, luscious and seductive, and great for chocolate lovers. It's important, though, to get the proportions right so that the brandy stands out as the major investor.

stinger

2 oz. brandy
1 oz. crème de menthe (white)

Shake the ingredients together over ice and strain into a frosted martini glass.

The **Stinger** is a great palate cleanser and digestif and, like brandy, should be consumed after dinner. The amount of crème de menthe added depends on personal taste. The **Sidecar**, like many of the classic cocktails created in the 1920s, is attributed to the inventive genius of Harry MacElhone, who founded Harry's New York Bar in Paris. It is said to have been created in honor of an eccentric military man who would roll up outside the bar in the sidecar of his chauffeur-driven motorcycle. It is certainly the cocktail choice of people who know precisely what they want.

2 oz. brandy
juice of half a lemon
½ oz. Cointreau

Shake all the ingredients
together over ice and strain
into a frosted martini glass
with a sugared rim.

sidecar

1 oz. Campari
1 oz. sweet vermouth
club soda
1 orange slice

Build the ingredients over ice
into a highball glass, stir, and
serve with an orange slice.

americano

The **Americano** and the **Negroni** have, of course, been around for a long time. The Americano is a refreshing blend of bitter and sweet, topped with club soda to make the perfect thirst quencher for a hot summer afternoon. The Negroni packs a powerful punch, but still makes an elegant aperitif. For a drier variation, add a little more dry gin, but if a fruity cocktail is more to your taste, wipe some orange zest around the top of the glass and add some to the drink.

negroni

1 oz. Campari
1 oz. sweet vermouth
1 oz. gin
orange zest

Build all the ingredients into a rocks glass filled with ice, garnish with a twist of orange zest, and stir well. For an extra-dry Negroni, add a little more gin.

The **Golden Cadillac** is not a drink to be approached lightly, and you could be excused for raising your eyebrows at the possibility of mixing crème de cacao (chocolate-flavored) with orange juice and Galliano (herb and licorice-flavored.) If the thought of this combination is too much for you, try substituting the crème de cacao with Cointreau to create another popular cocktail called Golden Dream. The **Grasshopper** is a more obvious combination of peppermint and cream, the perfect drink for after dinner.

golden
cadillac

1 oz. crème de cacao (white)
1 oz. light cream
2 oz. fresh orange juice
a dash of Galliano

Shake all the ingredients over ice, strain into a martini glass, and serve.

grasshopper

1 oz. crème de menthe (white)
½ oz. crème de menthe (green)
½ oz. light cream

Shake all the ingredients over ice, strain into a frosted martini glass, and serve.

CHAMPAGNE

1 oz. brandy
1 white sugar cube
2 dashes of Angostura bitters
dry champagne

Moisten the sugar cube with
Angostura bitters and place in
a champagne flute. Add the
brandy, then gently pour in
the champagne and serve.

champagne
cocktail

This cocktail has truly stood the test of time,

as popular now as when it was sipped by

the stars of the silver screen in the 1940s.

It's a simple and delicious cocktail that

epitomizes the elegance and sophistication

of that era and still lends that same touch of

urbanity to those who drink it today.

If there is another drink in the world that looks more tempting and drinkable than a **Black Velvet**, then please, someone make it for me now. Pour this drink gently into the glass to allow for the somewhat unpredictable nature of both the Guinness and the champagne. The **Bellini** originated in Harry's Bar in Venice in the early 1940s and became a favorite of the movers and shakers of chic society. Although there are many variations on this recipe, there is one golden rule for the perfect Bellini—always use fresh, ripe peaches to make the peach juice.

black
velvet

Guinness
champagne

Half-fill a champagne flute with Guinness, gently top with champagne, and serve.

bellini

¼ fresh peach, skinned
½ oz. crème de pèche
a dash of peach
    bitters (optional)
champagne
peach ball

Blend the peach and add
to a champagne flute.
Pour in the crème de pèche
and the peach bitters,
if using, and gently top up
with champagne, stirring
carefully and continuously.
Garnish with a peach ball
in the bottom of the glass,
then serve.

1 oz. vodka
1 white sugar cube
2 dashes of Angostura bitters
champagne

Moisten the sugar cube with
Angostura bitters and put it into
a martini glass. Cover the sugar
cube with the vodka and top
with champagne.

james bond

french 75

2 oz. gin
1 oz. fresh lemon juice
½ oz. sugar syrup
champagne
lemon zest

Shake the gin, lemon juice, and
sugar syrup over ice and strain
into a champagne flute. Top with
champagne and garnish with a
long strip of lemon zest.

The **James Bond** is a variation on the
Champagne Cocktail, using vodka instead
of the more traditional brandy. The naming
of this cocktail is a mystery to me since the
eponymous spy liked his drinks shaken!
The **French 75** is another classic cocktail from
Harry's New York Bar in Paris. It's not dissimilar
to a Gin Sling, but is topped up with champagne
instead of club soda.

index

CONVERSION CHART

Measures have been
rounded up or down slightly
to make measuring easier.

Imperial	Metric
½ oz.	12.5 ml
1 oz. (single)	25 ml
2 oz. (double)	50 ml
3 oz.	75 ml
4 oz.	100 ml
5 oz.	125 ml
6 oz.	150 ml
7 oz.	175 ml
8 oz.	200 ml